Adult Coloring

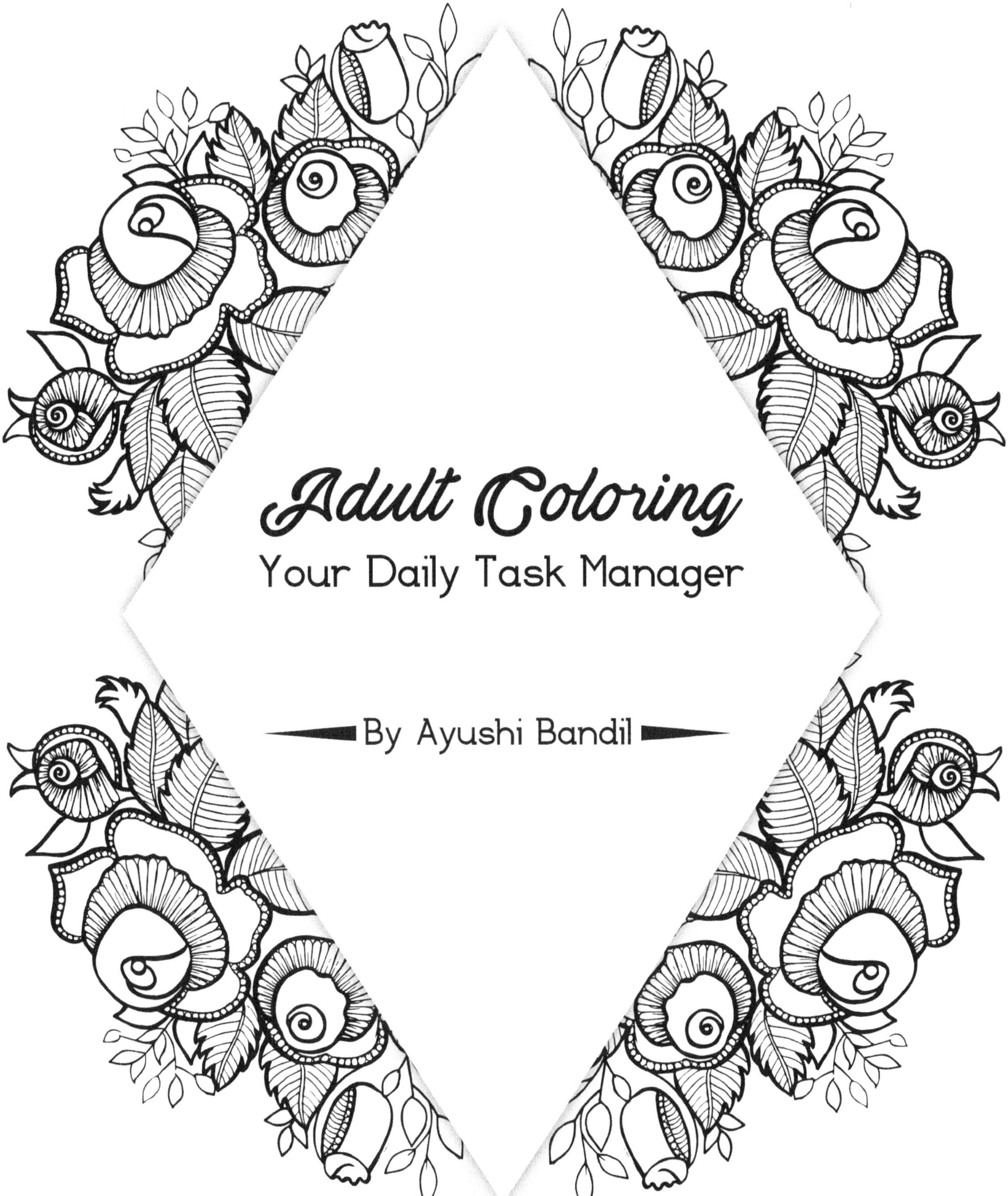

Your Daily Task Manager

◄ By Ayushi Bandil ►

ISBN-13:
978-1530730162

ISBN-10:
1530730163

Remember those childhood days when those nosy crayons used to cry out loud to see your inner artist? Those times when stress and anxiety were completely alien to you and you didn't have a muddled pile of tasks to manage.

Imagine! A book which can do both. Adult Coloring Book: Your Daily Task Manager not only brings back the nostalgia of revamping your childhood artist but also serves as a task manager for your scrambled daily tasks to meet your deadlines and be a step ahead of your competitors.

Coloring not only brings out creativity but also is the most effective stress-buster to be in a tranquil mood. Adult Coloring Book: You Daily Task Manager contains specially crafted real hand drawn illustrations drawn by pen and brush giving you a more realistic perspective to bring out your artist and the images come alive.

Real hand drawn illustrations! Cool. Isn't?

Let's dive into the world of creativity and portray your flamboyant imagination. And yeah! Never to worry about your topsy-turvy tasks.

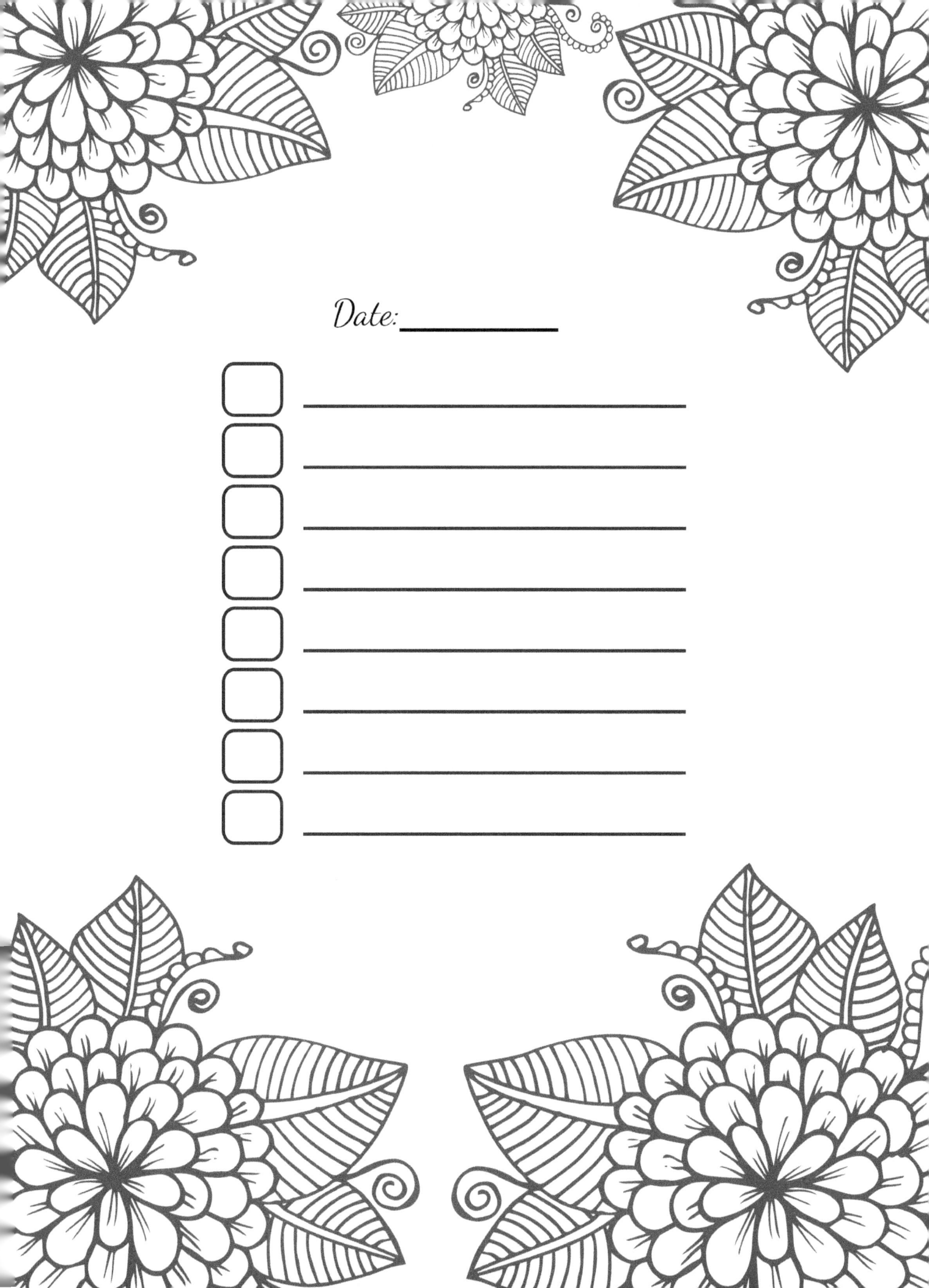

Date: _____

Date: _____

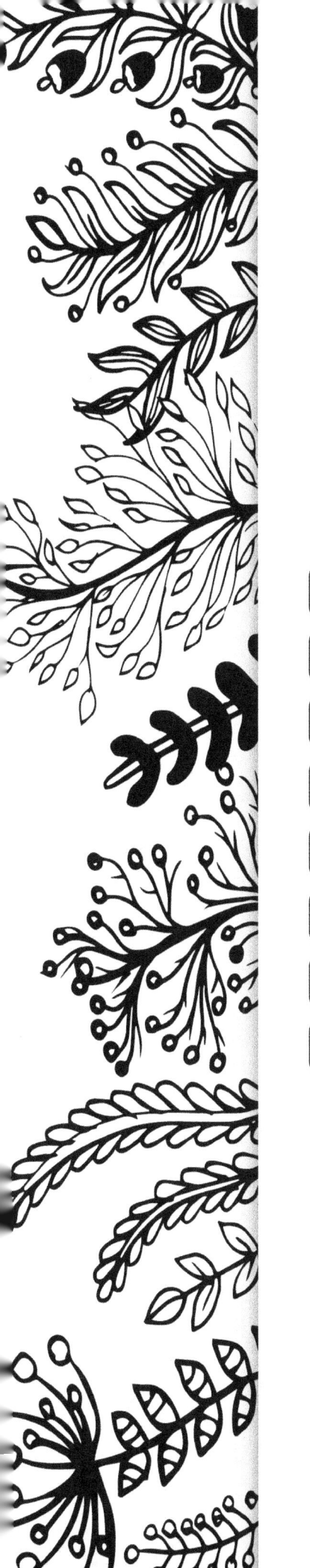

Date: _____

- [ ] _____
- [ ] _____
- [ ] _____
- [ ] _____
- [ ] _____
- [ ] _____
- [ ] _____
- [ ] _____

Date:_____

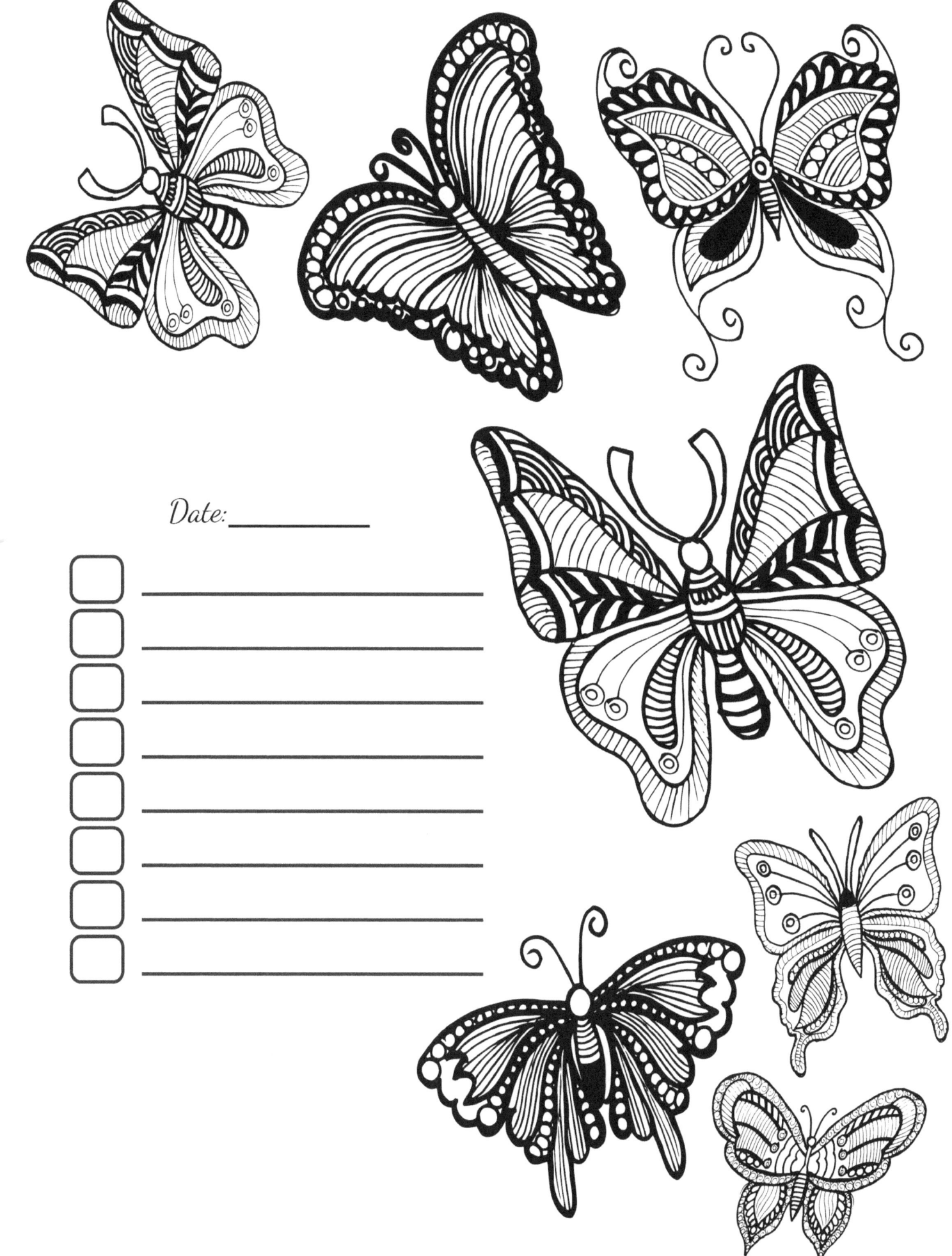

Date:_____

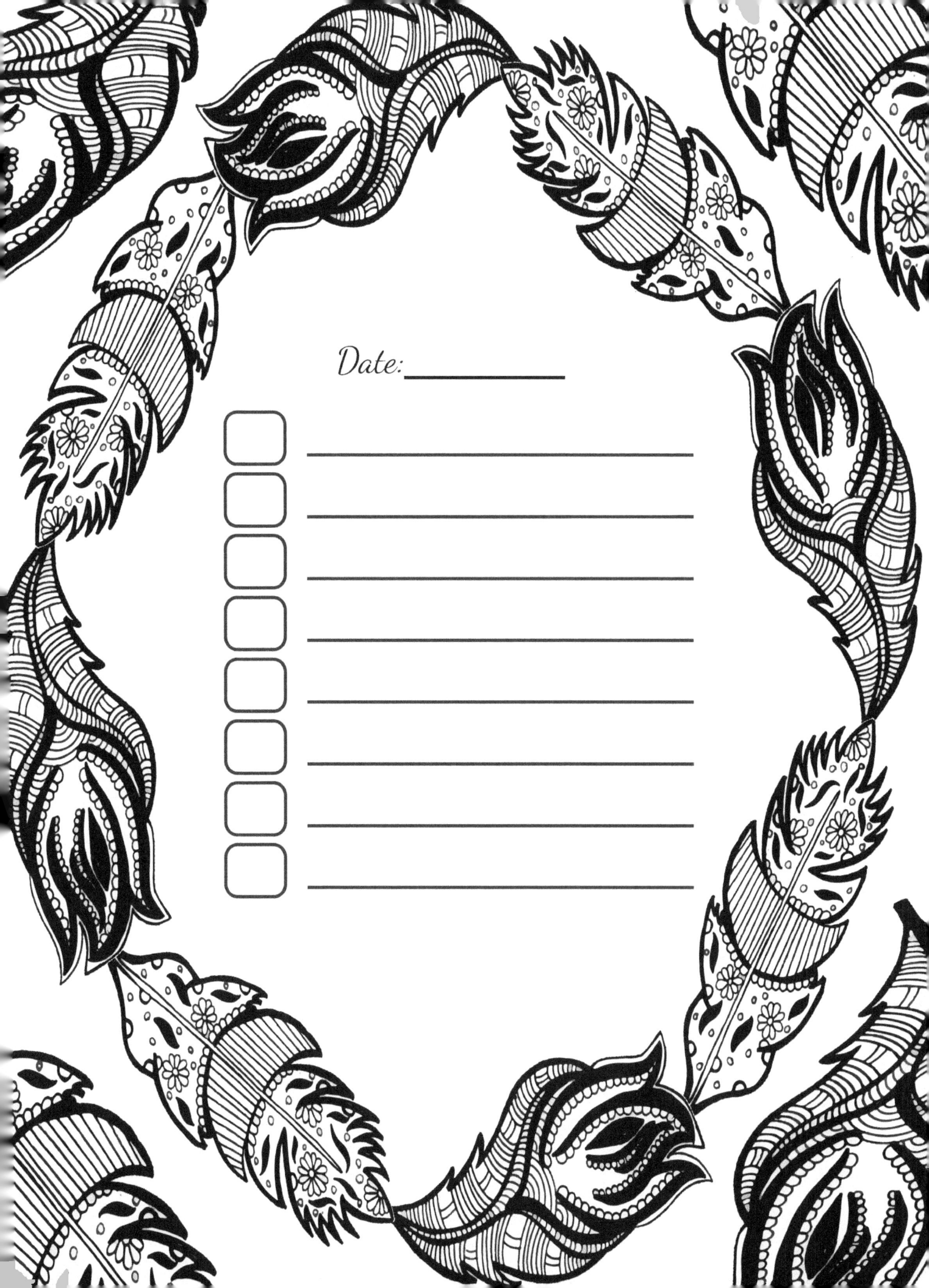

Date:_____

Date:_____

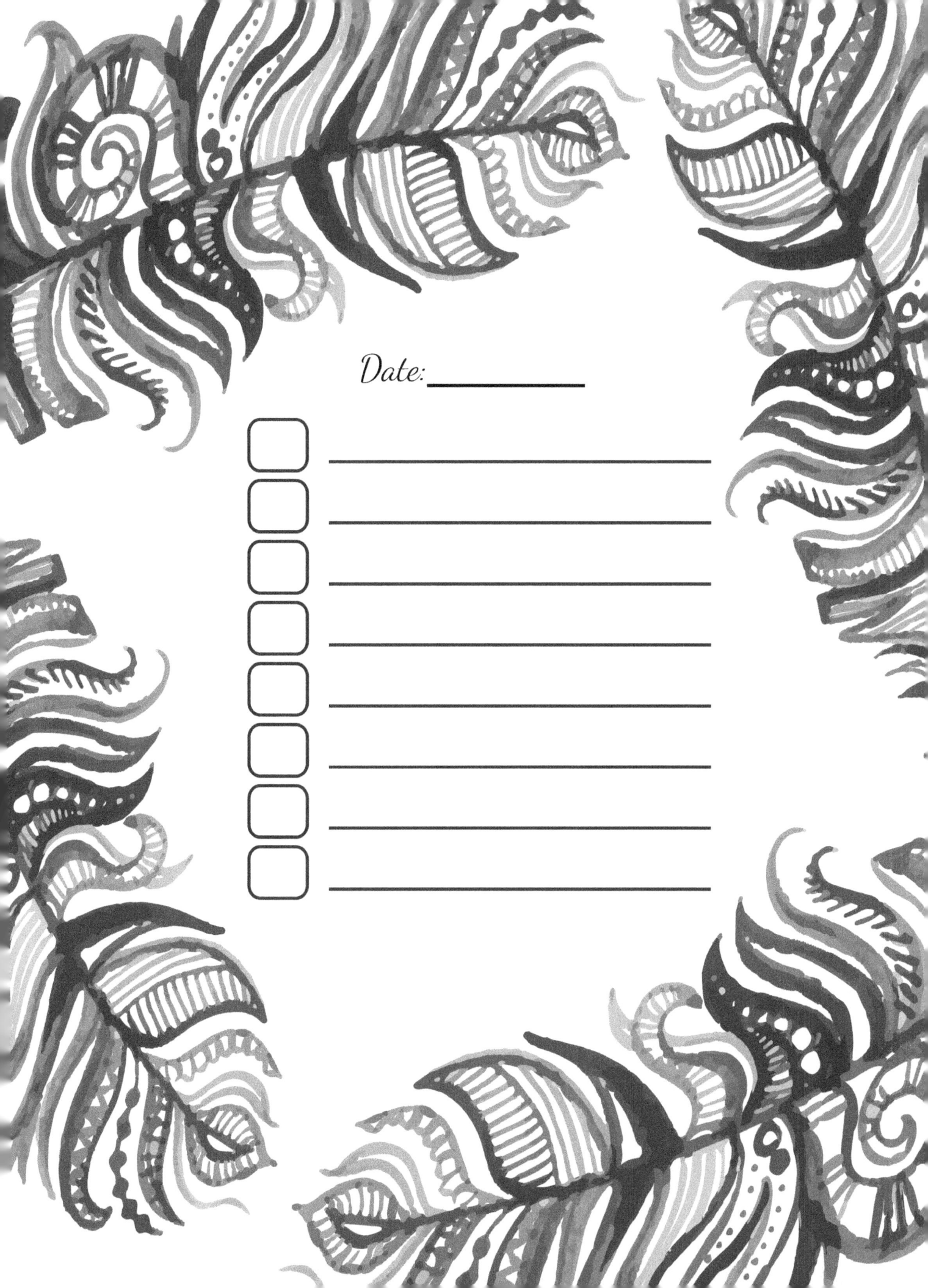

Date:_____

☐ _____

☐ _____

☐ _____

☐ _____

☐ _____

☐ _____

☐ _____

☐ _____

Date:_____

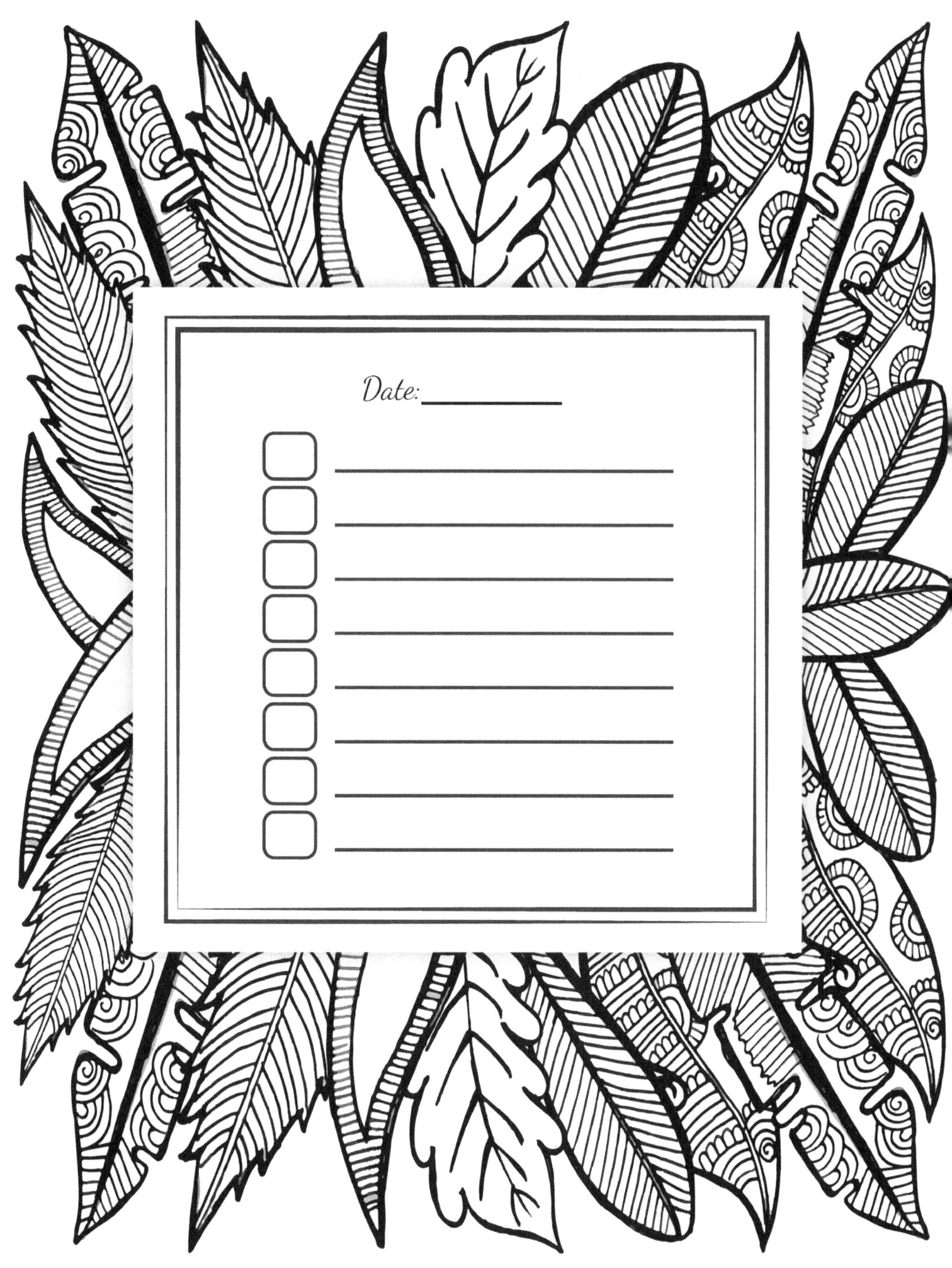

Date:_____

Date:_____

Date: _____

☐ _____
☐ _____
☐ _____
☐ _____
☐ _____
☐ _____
☐ _____
☐ _____

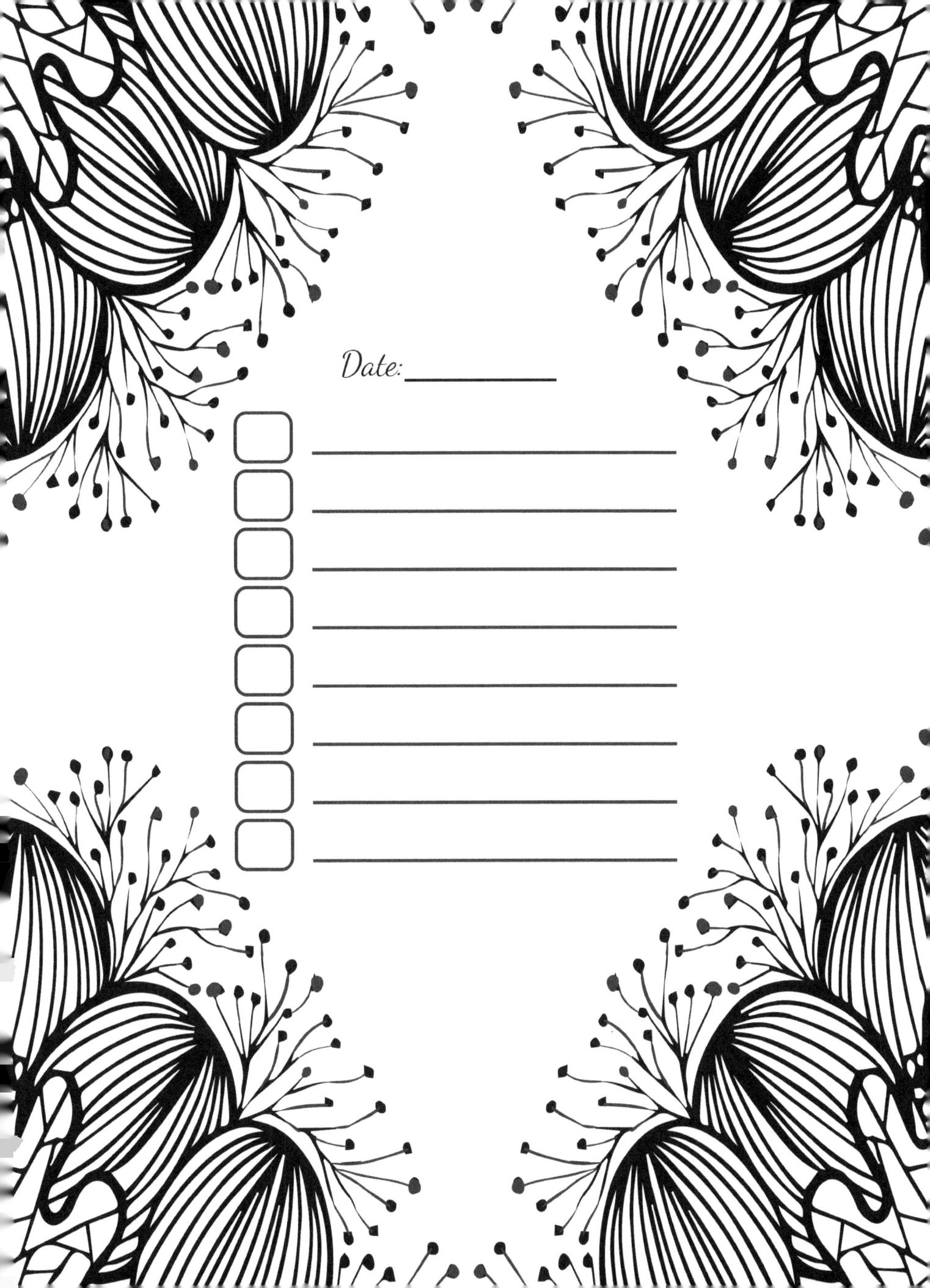

Date:_____

_____
_____
_____
_____
_____
_____
_____
_____

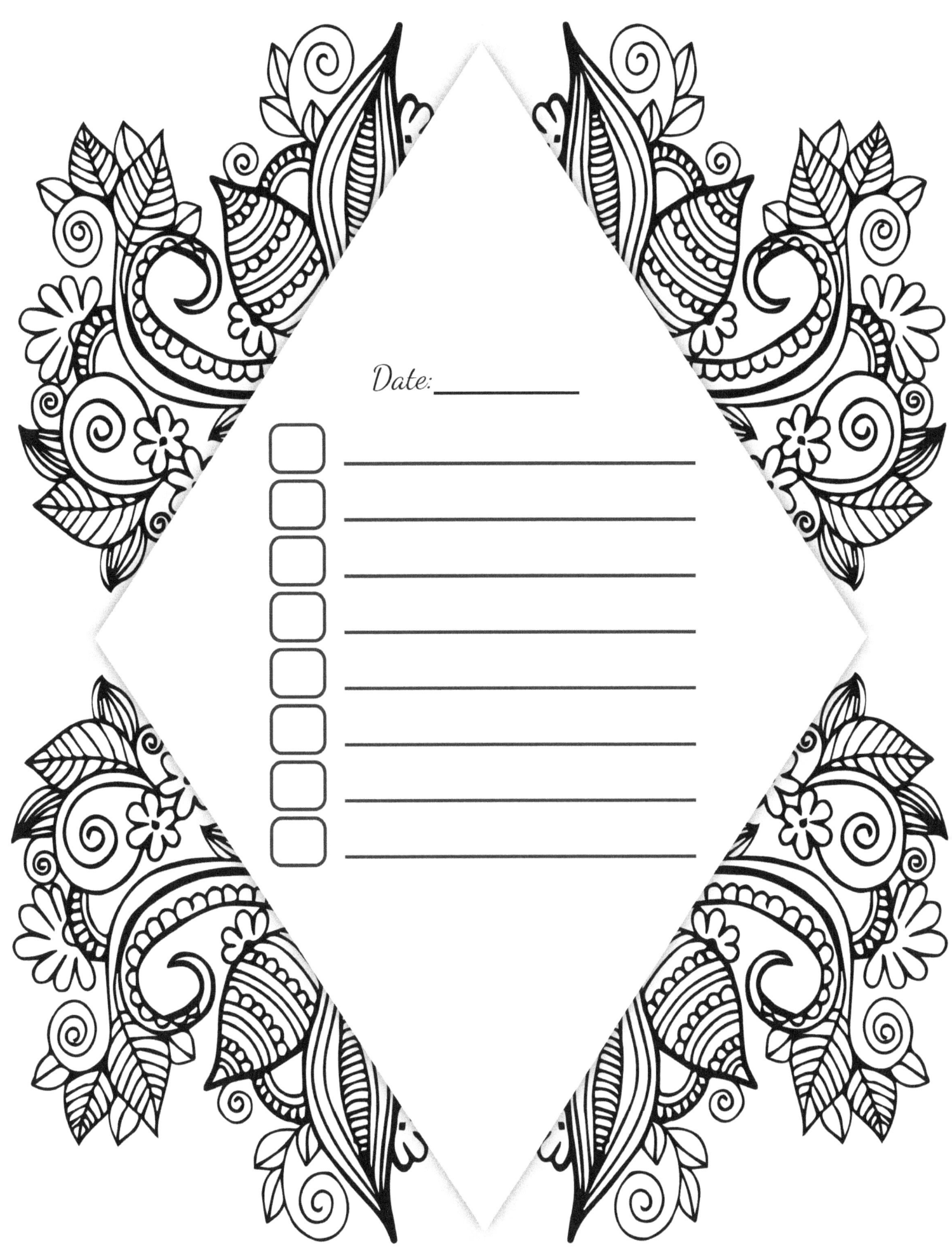

Date: _____

☐ _____
☐ _____
☐ _____
☐ _____
☐ _____
☐ _____
☐ _____
☐ _____
☐ _____

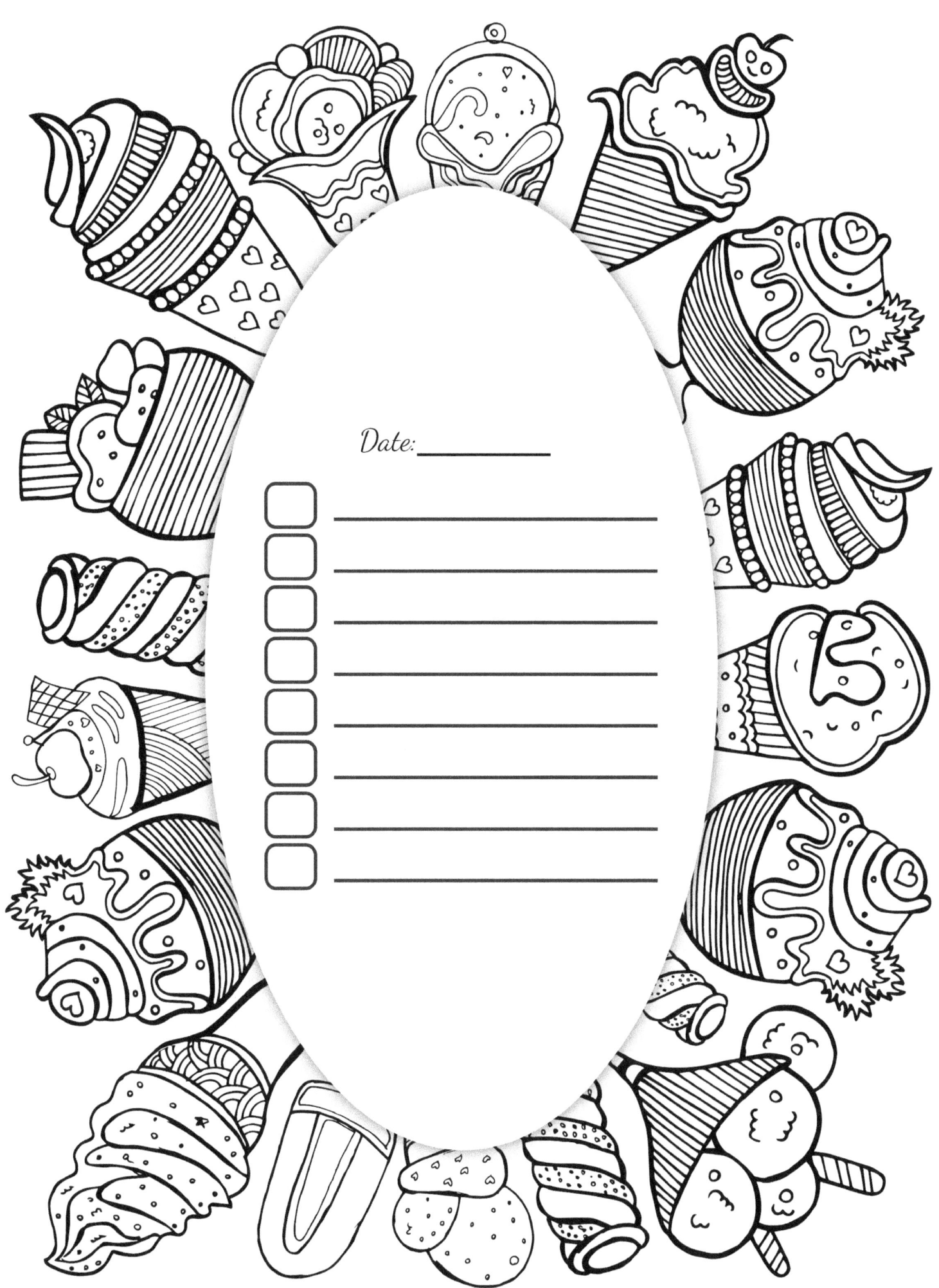

Date: _____

Date:_____

☐ _____

☐ _____

☐ _____

☐ _____

☐ _____

☐ _____

☐ _____

☐ _____

☐ _____

Date:_____

Date:_____

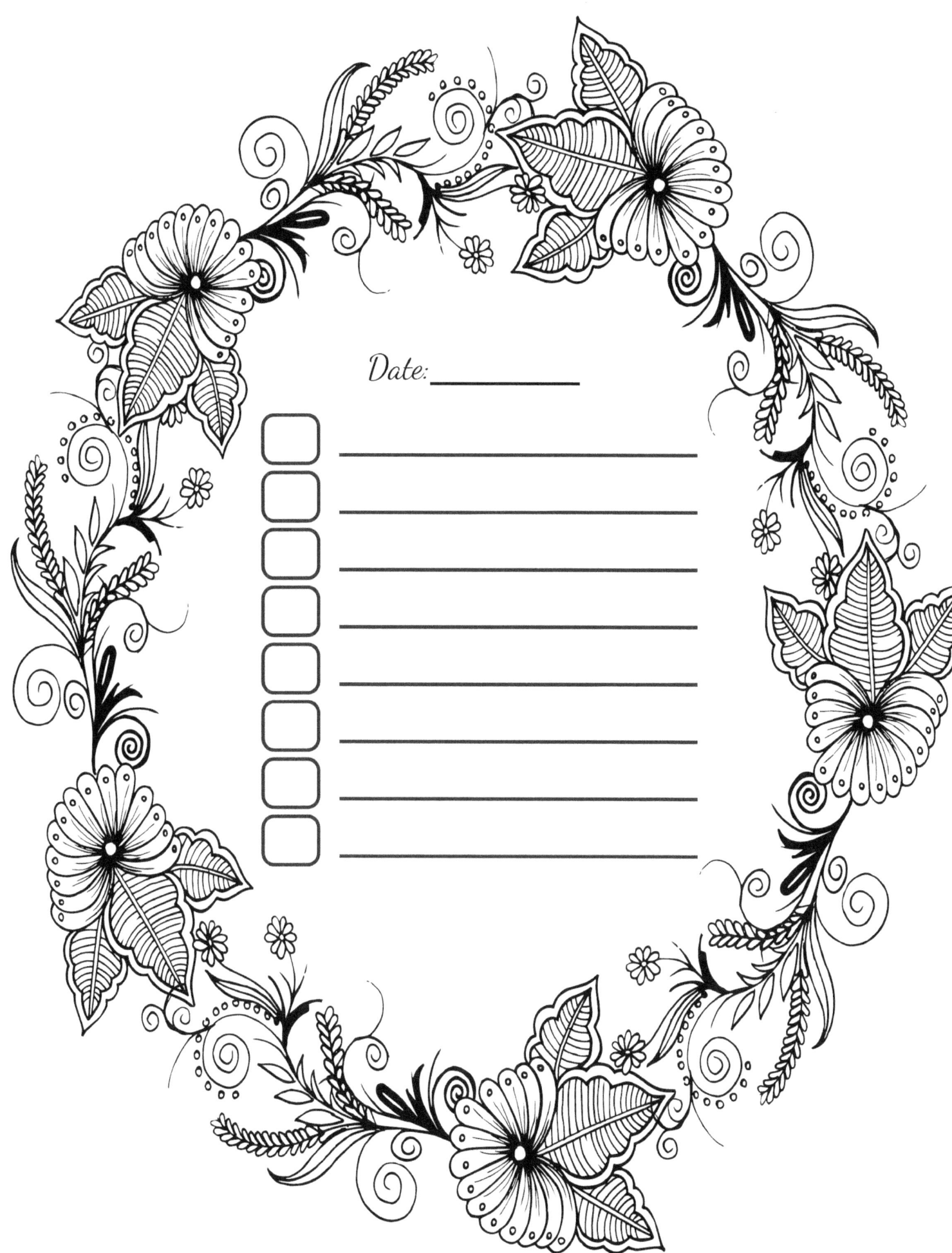

Date: _____

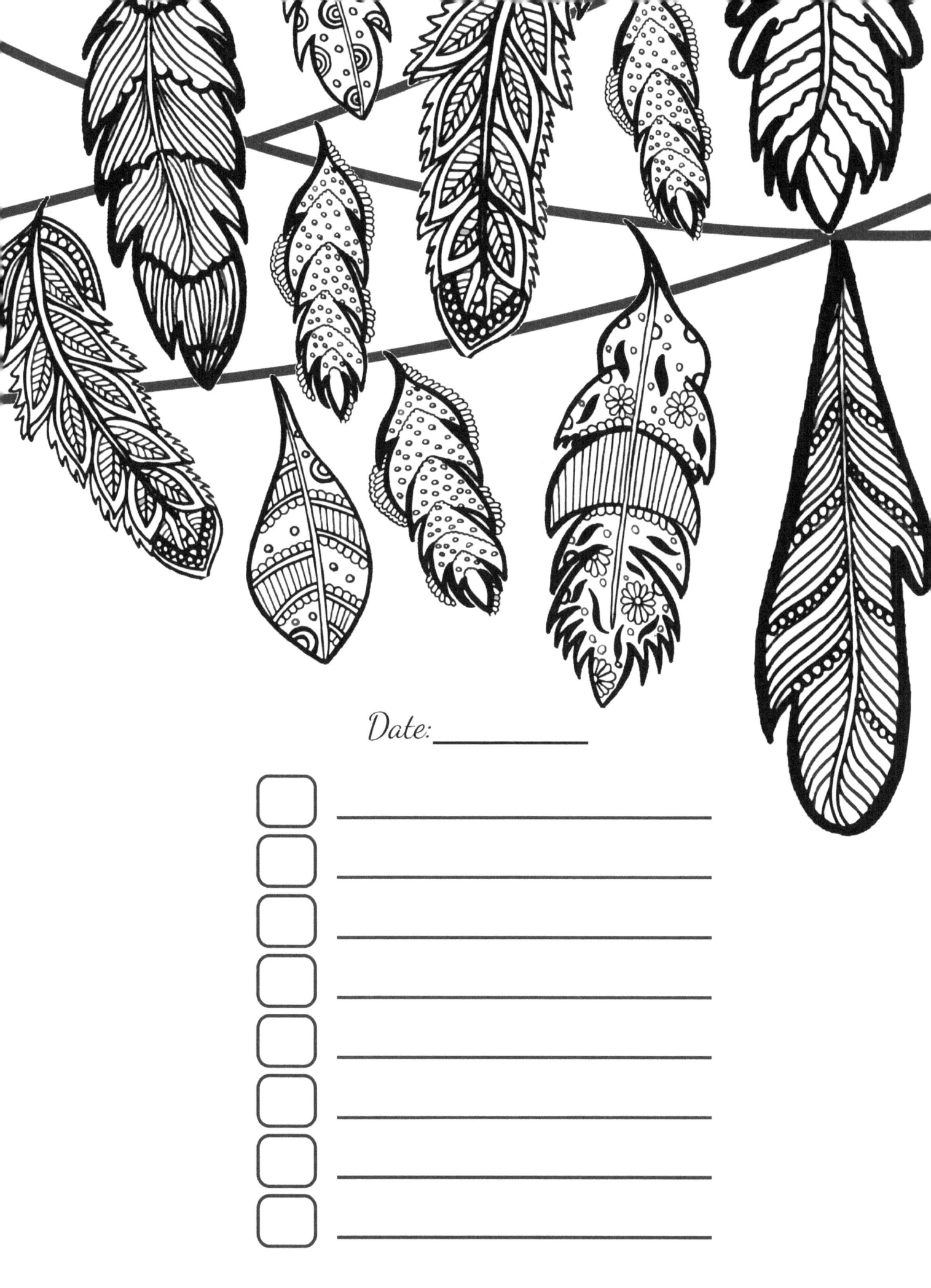

Date:_____

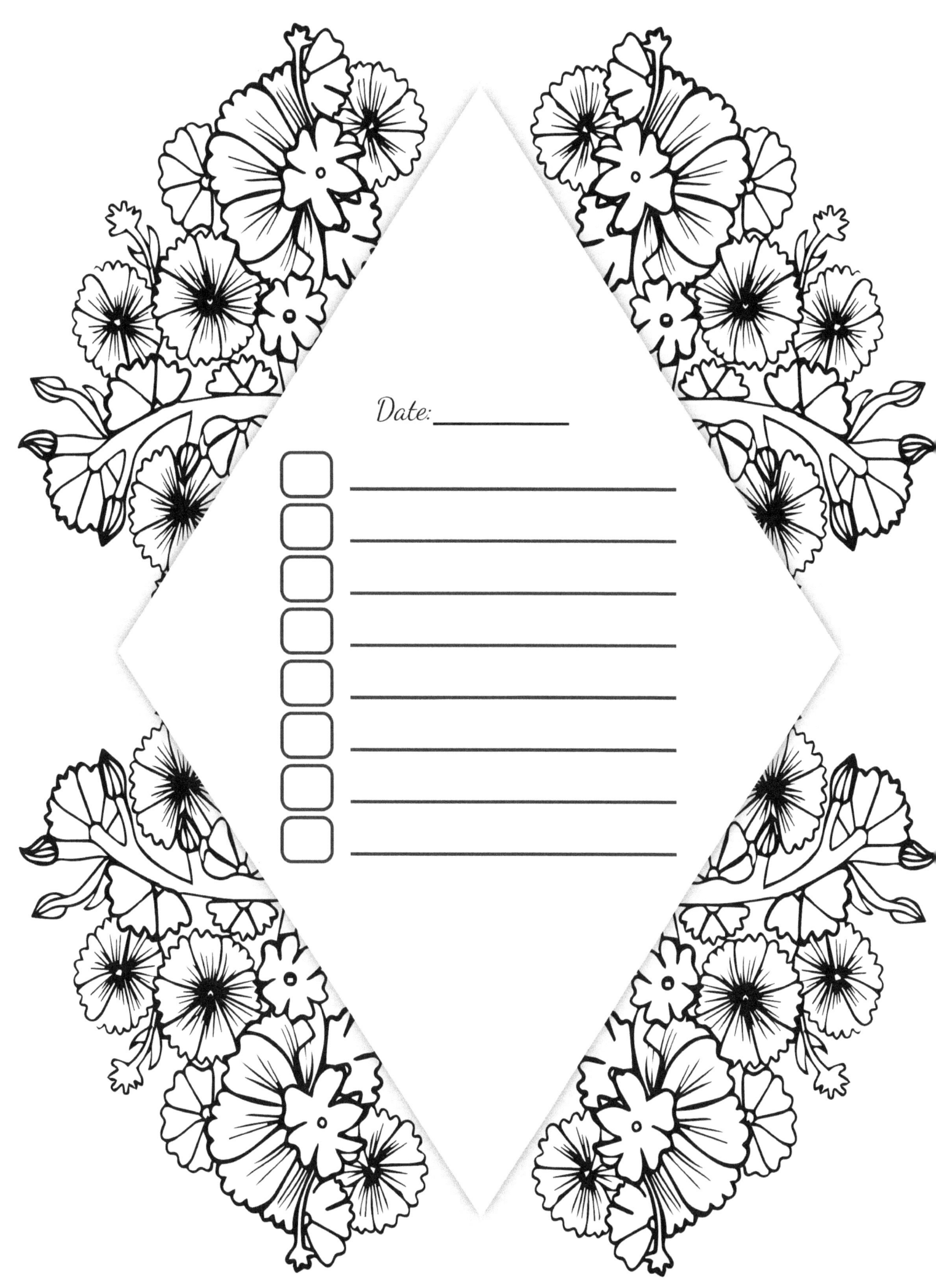

Date:_____

Date: _____

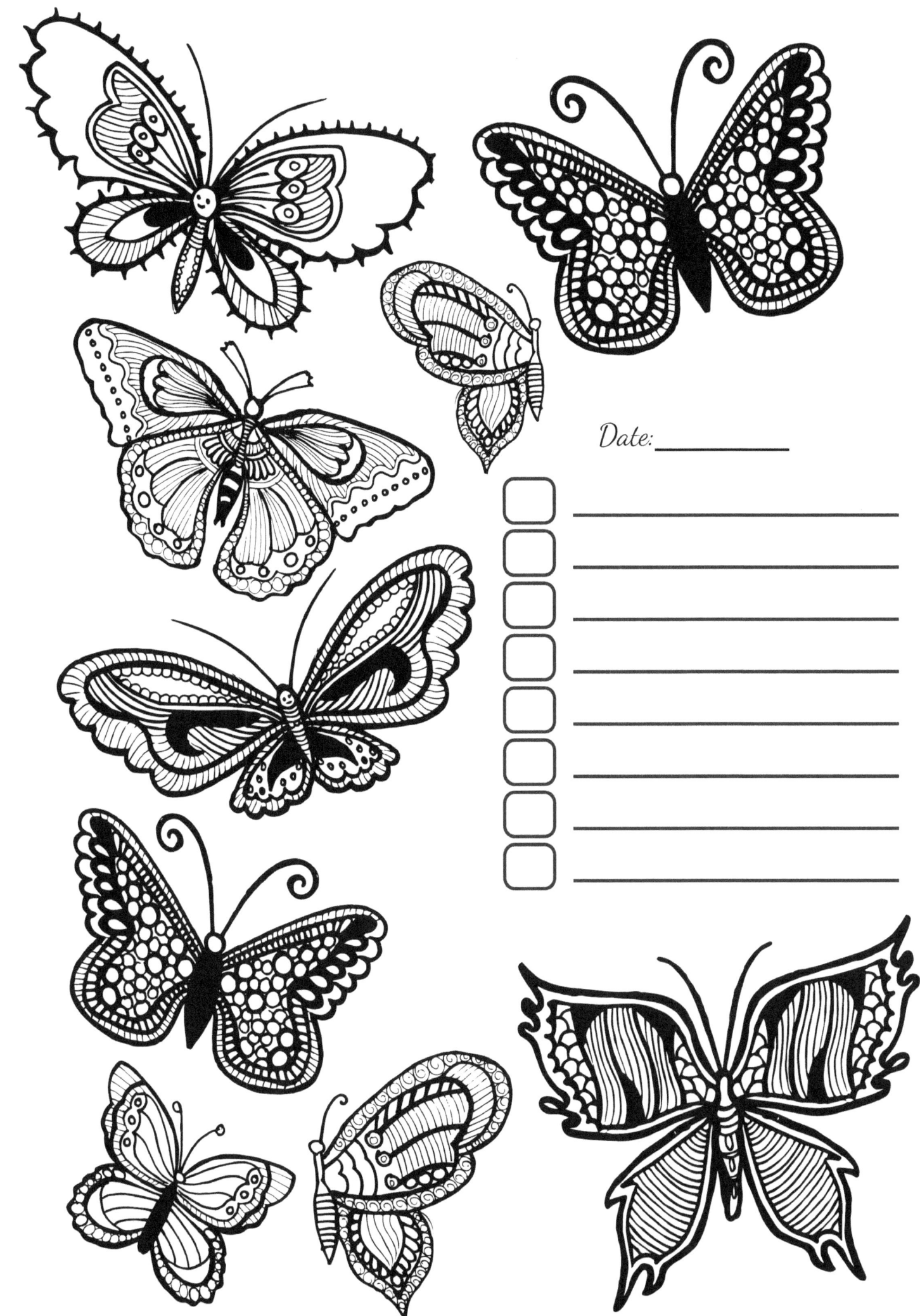

Date:_____

Date: _____

☐ _____
☐ _____
☐ _____
☐ _____
☐ _____
☐ _____
☐ _____
☐ _____

Date: _____

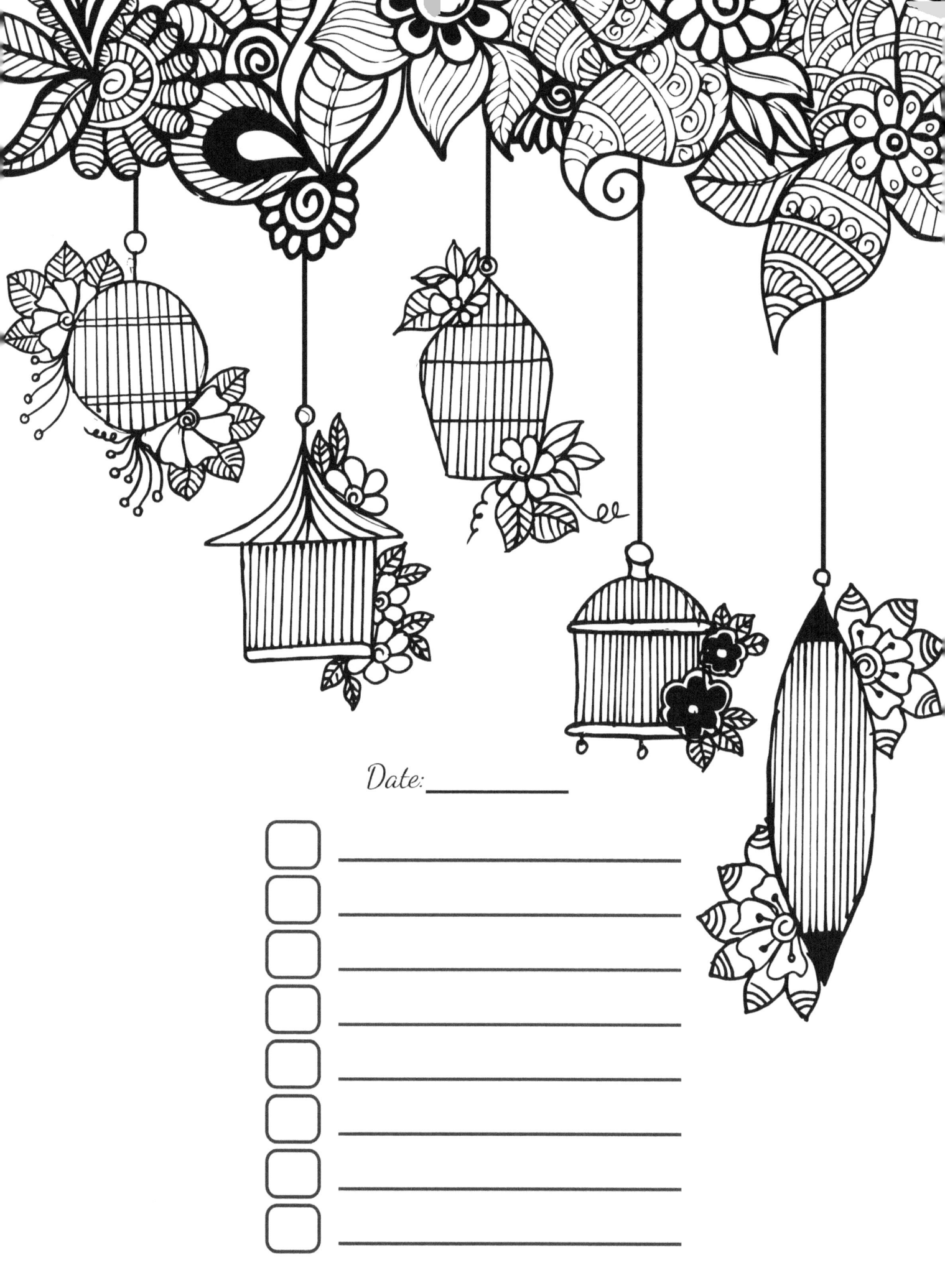

Date:_____

- ☐ _____
- ☐ _____
- ☐ _____
- ☐ _____
- ☐ _____
- ☐ _____
- ☐ _____
- ☐ _____
- ☐ _____

Date: _____

Date:_____

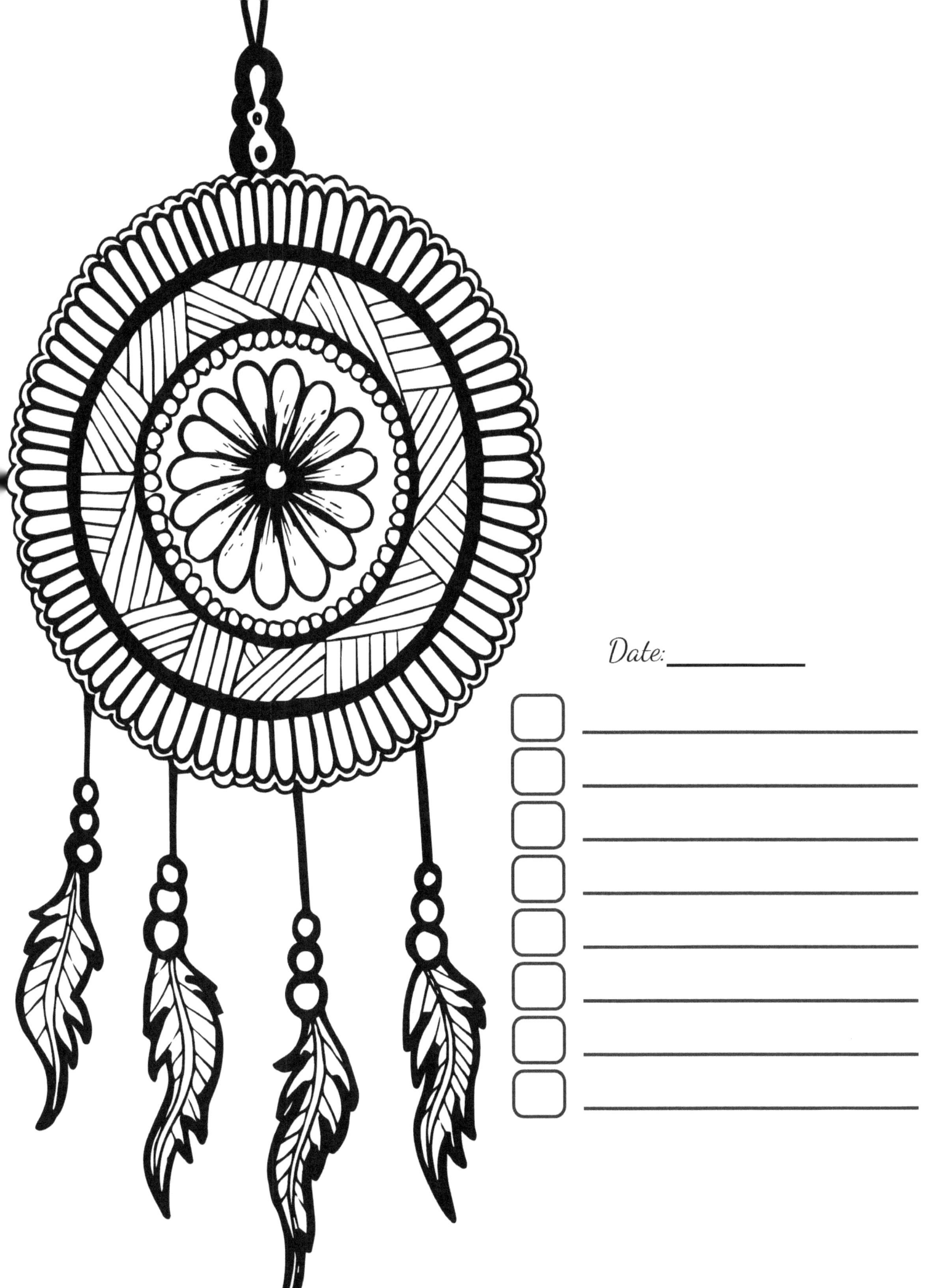

Date:_____

Date: _____

Date:_____

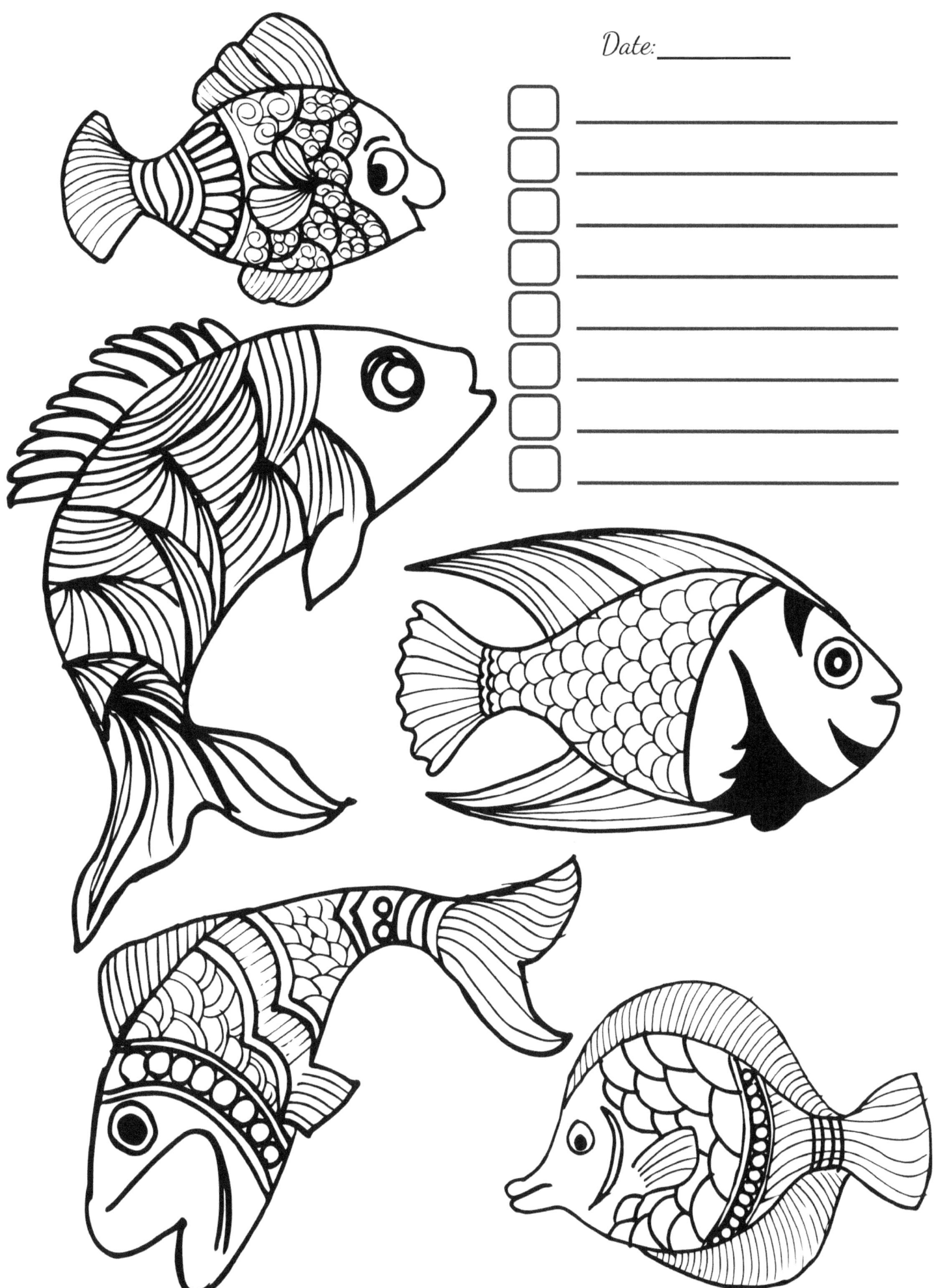

Date:_____

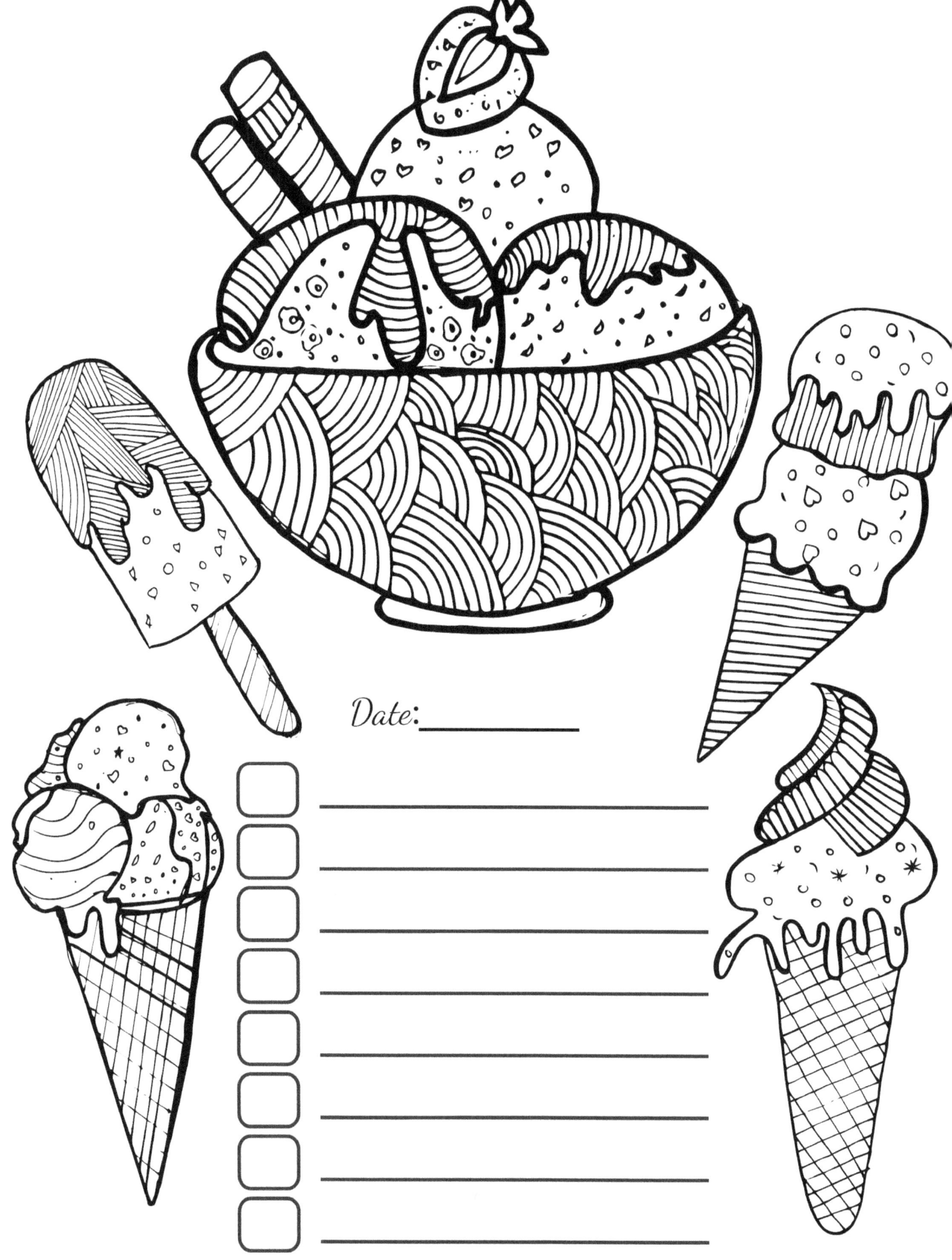

Date:_____

_____
_____
_____
_____
_____
_____
_____
_____

Date:_____

Date:_____

Date:_____

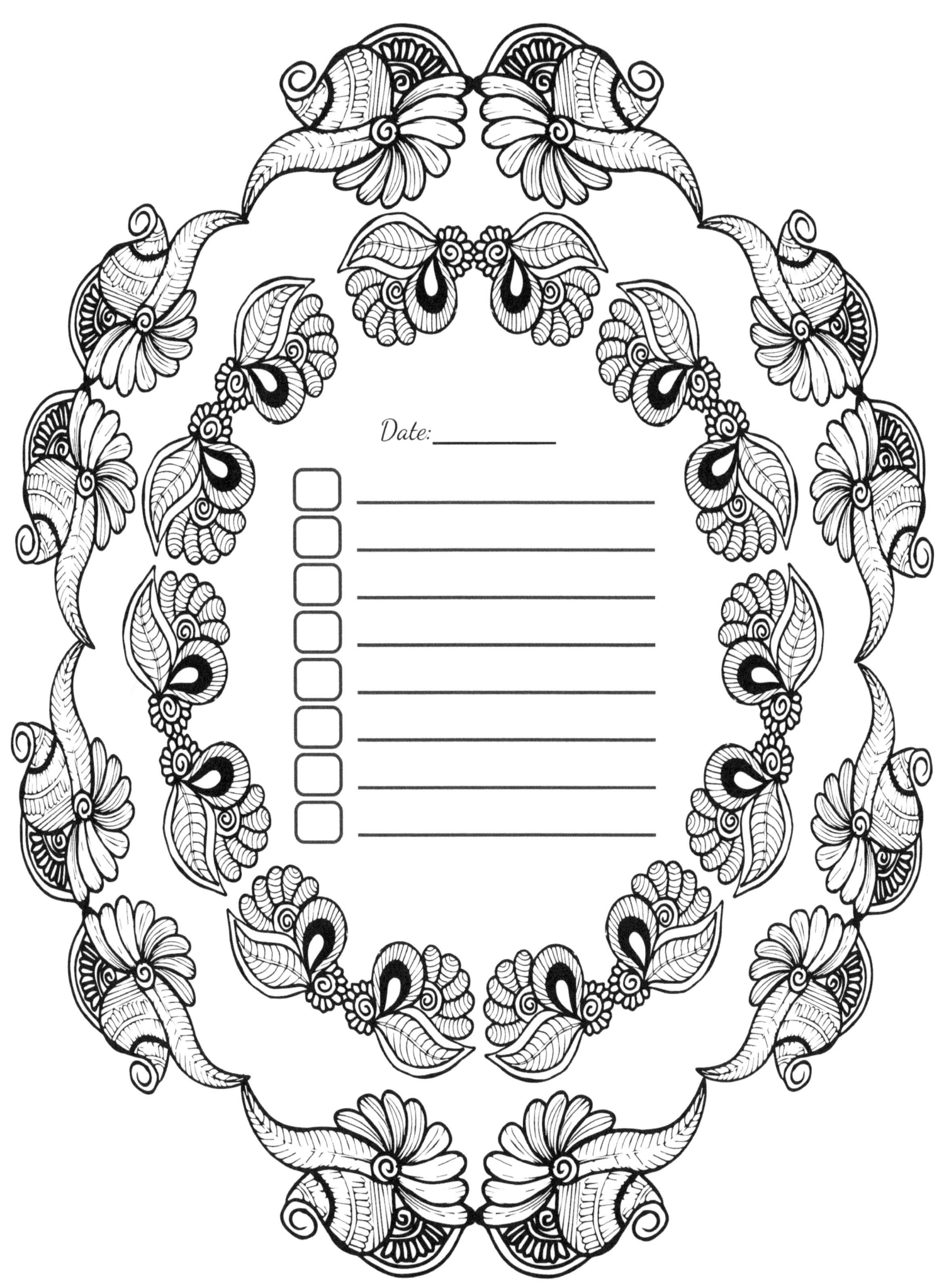

Date:_____

Date:_____

Date:_____

- [ ] _____
- [ ] _____
- [ ] _____
- [ ] _____
- [ ] _____
- [ ] _____
- [ ] _____
- [ ] _____
- [ ] _____

Date: _____

☐ _____

☐ _____

☐ _____

☐ _____

☐ _____

☐ _____

☐ _____

☐ _____

Did you like it?
Do provide your feedback ^_^

www.ingramcontent.com/pod-product-compliance
Lightning Source LLC
Chambersburg PA
CBHW080625190526
45169CB00009B/3292